T0105773

As I Remember
in Poetry and Prose

Natalia Finocchiaro

Order this book online at www.trafford.com
or email orders@trafford.com

Most Trafford titles are also available at major online book retailers.

© Copyright 2010 Natalia Finocchiaro.
All rights reserved. No part of this publication may be reproduced, stored in a retrieval system, or
transmitted, in any form or by any means, electronic, mechanical, photocopying, recording, or
otherwise, without the written prior permission of the author.

Printed in the United States of America.

ISBN: 978-1-4269-3367-7 (sc)
ISBN: 978-1-4269-3368-4 (e-b)

Library of Congress Control Number: 2010907741

*Our mission is to efficiently provide the world's finest, most comprehensive book publishing
service, enabling every author to experience success. To find out how to publish your book, your
way, and have it available worldwide, visit us online at www.trafford.com*

Trafford rev. 08/17/2010

 www.trafford.com

North America & international
toll-free: 1 888 232 4444 (USA & Canada)
phone: 250 383 6864 ♦ fax: 812 355 4082

Acknowledgments

Many thanks to my husband George for his unconditional love through all those years. I know how hard it was! My thanks to my psychiatrist, Dr. David Roane, for treating me so gently and always showing an interest in me and my work. It only encouraged me to do more. Many thanks from the heart and appreciation to my psychologist, Jill Daino, who has always encouraged me to write more, no matter what mood I was in. Even during the five years that I couldn't write, she insisted that I should put my feelings into writing. Many thanks to my two sons Karl Latendorf and Andrei Finocchiaro, my daughter-in-law Cindy Latendorf, and not forgetting my two grandchildren, Natasha and Karl Latendorf, for their support and love. Most of all, thank you to my brother Sergei Waisman, for coming every day while I was hospitalized. Without you I would have never made it; you brought me the outside world each day. Thank you.

Thank you all for your tremendous help.

Preface

This book of poems and prose came into being when I got sick and was diagnosed with bipolar disorder. I was at my worst when it came to my sickness. As a bipolar, I was hospitalized at least fifteen times between the years of 1986 and 2002. But these were my most productive years in my art field.

Everything seemed easy, and it was. Everything was intense and full of color, everyone was beautiful, and tremendous energy flowed in me. I was manic! I produced sixty-six paintings during my worst time, of which fifty-six are at large now. With all that energy my mind never stopped, not day or night.

The imagination soared, the memories had surfaced, I was happy, I was sad, I was high, I was low. But it was all nonstop.

I hallucinated, I did not sleep, I was manic, and I heard voices at times, day and night. But I never got tired.

I wrote during psychotic episodes and great depressions when finally my mind was at peace. Life experiences and memories from the past had surfaced and mingled with today's reality. I wrote some of these poems in the middle of the night when my mind wouldn't rest due to the voices in my mind, and some others during my many hospitalizations.

My imagination soared. It was vivid and exciting, sad and painful, full of love and longing. I drank, I smoked, and I attended rock concerts and rock performances that my son Andrei played in. I hung out with his group of friends. I made a lot of debts and lots of parties.

And all that time I worked, writing and painting.

And I drove everyone crazy!

My mind was a scramble. The voices, by now, were nonstop, but I would stop taking the medication and wind up in the hospital once more. It was hard to diagnose me. I seemed normal, just talkative and very happy. I was the only one who knew that I was sick. It was my secret.

In 2002 I had a big relapse in my illness and had to be hospitalized for three months. I was put on a high dose of medication. For fear of recurrence, I continued to take it religiously, but it numbed my senses. The medication desensitized me, and I was not the same.

Without the medication, everything was beautiful and everyone was beautiful. I was in love with love.

Now hard reality set in.

After five years of struggle with myself it came to pass.

My doctor reduced my medication.

Now I saw the world again through different eyes and mind.

Now I was at peace and could go on.

I fell in love again with every thing I saw and did.

Loving, caring people surrounded me.

How mighty and how great you are.
How lucky have I been, how blessed,
that you bestowed upon me
not one talent but two—
the painting and the writing.
　　Thank you.

Contents

A Letter Never Sent—1962

Dear friends back home, I write to you with sadness in my heart, and happiness too. It's gray out here. It's all cement around; no mountain or trees out here, no flowers to be picked, no wild grapes, no trails to walk so free to near and far, no water from ancient springs that's cool and clear to quench your thirst on hot summer's days. It is all gray, my dearest friends; why was I brought out here?

There is sand and ocean near my house where I do live. I walk long walks collecting shells, and only when I don't work, I miss you all. The flower, dearest friend, I miss you most, the nights we sat under the starry skies in conversations, the long card games and dances at the club and dancing in the streets, and most of all I miss the warm desert breeze, but I must confess something I must not withhold from you—I was introduced to someone new today.

Tall, black haired, blue eyes, and of fair skin he is, a god, believe me when I tell you, a god he is. His name is strange; it's after a false saint, it is. I should have bowed to him but I have only stretched my hand.

1964 to 1972

To school I have returned in morning but new.
An artist I'll be; my dream will come true.
To an island I'll sail like Gauguin and I'll paint;
To Provence and to Spain and I'll just paint and paint
and one day a new student came in, a former cadet,
fairer than fair was he, big brown eyes had he.
Chums we became and running around we did
and dating we started bit by bit like new.
Somehow I overcame fear of abandonment now.
Lovers and friends we became, jealously guarded my game.
A miracle happened once more in my life.
He stood and declared as proud as could be, *It is I, the father to be,*
Gallant, my fair knight was he in his youth.
I dressed in a light blue lacy dress; he gave red roses to put.
Not to church we did go, but to the reverend's house,
black reverend blessed us in union and peace be our way.
A pretty ring was put on my finger that day and we kissed.
The papers were signed and handed to me.
A feast we had like Vikings on a wedding day on lobster and beer.
We lived in great peace harmony and friendship.
The papoose was with us far and near as we went our way.
The buttercup flower was I. and morning dew. too
until one day he decided to fly and spread wings,
wings of a plane that he followed some of his own that he grew.
I touched some else's arm by mistake and suddenly all was new.
Another bonnet, this time a green one with wings,
A green uniform, but he had a plaid pleated skirt too, and a crest.
The only sad part, that I knew he belonged to someone I knew.
My mind was a torch and started too long for someone.
The love that I once knew, he never left my mind or heart.
I blamed everyone. I cried, I got sick, I drank, and I left,
but the love never left. Into a hospital I was put.
For a summer I stayed. I forgot what I was or even who,
and now I was all over new like someone else.
The only one whom I knew was my son whom I loved.
No memories, no pain. To work once again I went,
dated here, dated there, but no one to love that I knew,
no love in my heart, in my mind, no love for anyone.
Sometimes I recollected black hair and blue eyes
in a light manner that was strange and new for the most part,
and slowly it crept—not the languages I lost

but the image I knew would make my heart beat faster.
But why I would think some things are so strange?
I started to think of the god that I met and once I knew.

The Miserable Ones

Greed, greed
Hate, hate
Envy, envy
These are the ruts of a miserable family
They dwell upon this earth among us
Unnoticed by most
Their hearts ache
Their souls tormented
To no avail
All else blamed for their unhappiness
They point discriminating finger and accusing eyes
Not only to those who are content without life's riches
But for those who have as well
They sit and wait and dwell in misery
That they create themselves
Tormented souls
Tormented minds
You are the vermin upon this earth
Not God's creation!
But your own
This life you live in rot
Wishing hate and misfortune to those you choose to envy
Will only bring misfortune upon your family
Make haste to make peace upon your souls
Or all your life is lost in eternal limbo
Tormented souls
Tormented bodies
Lost for all to see
But you yourself that love to dwell in such unhappy miseries
Create your own hell for all eternity

1986

The Promise

Let your future shine
Like the sun in June
Let there be no tears or fears
If you believe me,
It will pass just like all the winds
Chin up, head up
The future is for you
It's full of hopes and promise
There is no place on earth like here
Reach out as far as there,
But never say where
Just stride ahead
And your reward be gladness
It's sunshine all the way
Believe me, I went that way

1986

It's Only the Beginning

Stretch your arms
Straighten your knees
Foot ahead in front of me
Listen carefully; hear it all
Some may wish and want your fall
But keep that foot ahead of all
Think and listen
Look around
Feel
Make your move ahead so sudden
Like the thunder in the sky
Let them all see your stars
Grab your fortune
Let it shine
Youth has it all in mind
Don't look behind!

1986

Colors

My colors have been stolen
I don't know how, but they are gone
No one understands that I have lost my colors
My mind is a scramble—I must find all my colors

Who has stolen all my colors?
A tragedy occurred—I'm without my colors
I can't function—now my mind is a scramble
Where am I right now without my colors?

No one understands that I haven't got my colors
Who am I to accuse for stolen colors?
I must have my colors or I'll die
If you stole my colors, give them back to me

Without the colors I can't function well
My life revolves around colors
I must have my colors back or else
Please return all my colors or I'll die

My mind is inflamed with madness
Who has stolen all my color?
There is nothing left for me to do
I'm going mad without my colors

Madness has set in without the colors
I must have my colors back or I will die
Madness has set in while I'm looking for my colors
My mind is aflame—I'm going mad without the colors

Fire

My prince, my knight
Give me fire, fire, fire
I shall give you all desire
My prince aglow
My knight afire
Where has gone that cruel desire?
Give me fire, fire, fire
I shall give you all desire
All the youth that's gone aflame
All desire gone in vain

1986

The Hill of Peace

The hill of nothingness
The hill of peace and sleep
The hill of nothingness
Where dead are laid asleep
High up in the mountain
Where dead are laid at peace
Imposing birch trees overlooking all
They stand like guards
Like faithful soldiers on that hill
Reminding us of all that was and gone
The hopes, the pain
The laughter of years gone by
Someone had placed a flower
Someone had spilled a tear
The dead are sleeping in their peace
The living cry and hope
That no one will place them on the hill of nothingness
They leave in hopes of living for eternity to come
The birch trees know and wait
Silently they stand
Just waiting for someone to greet
The peaceful sleep—forever is so silent
You only hear the wind

1986

A Job at a UN Party in Jerusalem

Fifteen I am; a job I got, exciting job I got—a job to tend a bar and drinks to mix, just drinks—no mingling, no talking to the men, not one—just pour the liquor into glass at their request. Just pour it over ice or put some water tonic soda. No talking to the men I'm told, no talking to anyone. A job so easy for peace, a party, a party for good cause. All men, no ladies hanging on their arms to be held. A room, a separate room for drinks, where I have to stay alone. The men come in, I pour, and they depart to mingle.

A job I got, so cool, a bar maiden I am tonight. Behind a table I am standing while I pour the drinks. A tall man—blue eyes, dark-haired—approached with a smile.

Scotch please I'm told *just ice please* and he points. White shirt blue stripes no tie; a button is unbuttoned. *How old are you?* Fifteen I am, I tell with pride. Another man approaches—*gin please, ice and tonic.* A smile; *How old are you?* the other gentleman had asked.

Fifteen she is, a job she got, just for tonight, no hands. The other man just looks—white shirt, a tie, he smiles. *No mingling, I say, fifteen she is, let's go inside right now.* A smile from blue eyes, a second look at me, a nod. Fifty-four I am and I remember you, the smile and the nod, the white shirt blue stripes the top button undone short glass in hand, the noise from the inner party room—alone I stood, the music played.

A job I had, exciting job just for a night; fifteen I was, so proud A warm night, no air-conditioning at all, just desert summer breeze.

The Red Ruby

O Katarina, Katarina, Grandmother Katarina,
how I loved you beyond measure, beyond life itself

O Grandmother O Grandmother, why must I part from you?
You gave me an old ring with a pear-shaped ruby

O Grandmother Katarina, how I remember what you said:
Keep this ring of ruby to remember me by

O Grandmother Katarina, forgive me for disobeying
I wore the pear-shaped ruby ring

O dearest Grandmother, how much I loved the ring of ruby
I wore it on my middle finger with a lot of pride

O Grandmother, you must know how it feels
You loved your husband as I remember

O dearest, please forgive me for removing the ring from my finger
He put the pear-shaped ruby ring on his pinky finger

O dear Grandmother Katarina, he promised it was just a loan
But dearest Katarina, I have never seen him anymore

O dearest, O dearest, I have tried to retrieve it
But there was no ruby ring, no soldier in red beret

O Grandmother Katarina, he wore a pair of wings
No one could find my soldier that used the wings or had my ring

O Grandmother Katarina, please forgive me for the loss
I shall always remember you even without the pear-shaped ruby ring

O would I ever forget the soldier with the red beret and wings?
He stole the pear-shaped ruby ring, my dearest Katarina

My Creative Soul is Misunderstood

With each waking morning the thought is always the same: create.
The urgency of creation never leaves my side.
My argument inside my head: why paint, why write?
It is not bitterness or a regret or want of fame

It's just a statement that I must make.
I want to leave a mark, a legacy for my descendants.
Why must I waste and give my work for nothing?
Why do they buy the work of others?

And yet they want my work for nothing.
They have the means; they are better off than I.
They always have suggestions—sell at the market, on the porch,
but give us what we like and want for nothing.

You see, once I had a friend I thought was an artist like myself,
but she denied the title of an artist or a painter to my being
by replying, *painting to you it means nothing but to me it's my life.*
My dear she said, *I couldn't live without it but you can.*

I wonder what she does, how and where today.
She was the most insulting woman that I knew when it came to one's aspirations.
She was one of those who wanted all for nothing too.
I worked for her one day in mixing colors and did some painting.

She had insulted me with pay as if nothing to speak of for my work.
Her argument was, *I make ten times more then you;*
you earn in one day at work a hundred and I a thousand.
I do not care for pay or price for my creations, but not unworthy humiliation.

All I ask is please collect it; it's precious and unique; it's part of me
and all I want to do is leave a legacy of mine to my descendants.
Sadness overtakes me when I have no imagination or inspiration.
Desperation and unhappiness hover all around me like dark clouds.

Where is my imagination, where is my expression of my soul with such dark words?
And then with dawn I wake to color and sound of nature stirs my soul, and all else is forgotten.
My day begins, the urge returns to create in full color. Insipid is my thought that I have no worth.
My soul returned to me from sadness, darkness to sunshine and warmth toward mankind.

I'm alive—the colors are mine and mine alone on this earth.
Ideas flow—the love of creation is here again to stay for a while.
Exquisite that feeling and the argument ends in my mind for a short time.
I'll pick up a brush, swirl it in some color, and dab it slowly onto my canvas.

My Beloved King of Kings

To my most beloved David, of all the kings that were,
my admiration and love for you abound eternally in flames.
You were the Godly king and still are, now you are,
forever you remain the one eternal love of all,
beloved king, beloved love to all eternal life.
Your light guides my ways from near and far.
Beloved king of all, you are beloved to eternity to come.
The stars above have shone on you, the sun gave its rays.
You are the fire in the fields, you are the fire in the skies.
To God you sang; his pardon you have asked,
and yet you were the chosen one to guide and love.
You thought that you betrayed him in some strange sin,
but beloved king, all was forgiven then for you.
My dearest, most beloved King David you are.
Strange were your ways, strange were your thoughts.
You did not know that you were chosen as the loved one.
A diadem he gave you to put upon your head to lead;
a king he made you because he loved you as his own.
You have lamented to his name in happiness and sorrow.
The chosen one, you are as you are still now.
Beloved king of kings, you have compared your strength
to trees that grow to innermost height to succeed.
You are the chosen one and known to the tribe of Israel,
the king that was chosen to lead and worship in his grace,
O king of kings, beloved king David of Israel

Touched with Fire

O how quaint and nice it is to call us touched with fire,
those with the illness that afflicted so many in the arts from long ago.
Are we blessed, or are we condemned, by mental illness, or is it a disease?

No one can see it, or feel it except ourselves and our minds by affliction;
We are aware of it during the afflicted time that had taken hold.
No one can feel it, see it, or understand the feeling or the cause.

The writer called it touched with fire; whose fire is that touched my being?
Is it the gods from Mount Olympus, or is it from above somewhere?
Or maybe from between the worlds we live in, or from underworld somewhere.

Did God's hand touch us with its fire, or is it a torch inside,
The torch that burns in the darkness to lead all passersby and us?
How lucky and unlucky one can be, with such a fire in the mind?

I do not blame a soul, I do not complain, or cry, I do not ask even why
There must be a reason in this world that I am with such a fire
But my brothers were never touched with any fire in their minds.

Memories of my Mother in India

In the land of dust, sacred cows, and heat
There was a maharaja who wore a lovely turban on his head.
The turban was of lovely colors and bejeweled on its side.
He met his lovely lady with hazel almond eyes.
Her ways and grace bewildered him with passion.
He fell in love with that lovely lady and her children too.
He courted her and followed her around and proposed.
She flirted and she smiled and moved around him with grace.
They moved together from one city to the next
in that land of sacred cows and heat that is his own.
The children were adored by the maharaja with the turban
but the lovely lady with the hazel eyes was quite unsettled.
One day the time had arrived for that lovely lady to move on.
The maharaja with the colored bejeweled turban offered her a home:
We'll fly together just as one with your lovely children to a faraway land.
But the lovely lady thought awhile. Will she travel on
one day in a foreign country of round columns and graceful statues?
She answered *I part from you, dearest maharaja, and I go my way.*
He was heartbroken from her rejection and went on his way.
Not a year went by and he found her in the land of milk and honey.
He kept writing of his love and longing for her presence.
The letters were a song of love and poetry with praise to her alone
but the lovely lady with the hazel eyes did not reply.
The lovely lady kept those letters for some time and then they stopped.
One day another lover took those letters and destroyed them.
Only memories of the maharaja and the land of sacred cows remained.
Sometimes she thinks of all those times and of those lovely letters,
of her life gone by, her beauty vanished, but not her flirtatiousness and pride.

June 1999

To Sleep to Sleep to Sleep

To sleep forever and yet only to wake up each morning—
how shall I go to sleep forever, not to be awakened by someone,
to sleep forever, not to wake up at all, just sleep the deepest sleep?
How can I make sure that I will sleep and not awake each time,
just sleep without the wakening in the morning,
without the thought that occupies my mind,
without the pain that occupies my time,
without the tears that stream so easily each time?
How can I share my pain with someone?
How can I explain what goes on inside my mind?
Who will understand or who will ever care?
I sway like a weeping willow in the wind
each time that mood overtakes my mind.
Is there an end to it, is there a light somewhere to ease my mind?
I sway and sway like a branch of weeping willow,
until someday it will snap off in the wind
and maybe then the sleep will come to ease my mind,
just to wake up in the morning to see the sunshine,
no pain, no torment to the mind—just sunshine

October 30 1995

Tears, Streaming Tears

Tears for all the fears, for all the unknown
that awaits us somewhere out there,
those painful tears that stream—
they blur the vision, they wet the cheeks,
they pain the heart from sadness.
The aching heart cries in silence every day.
Those streaming tears, when nothing stops them.
They stream and stream, those tears.
A day goes by, a memory, a sound brings back the tears,
the tears for all that's lost, for all that's gone.
Is there a happy vision out there somewhere?
Is there some hope ahead out there,
something to stop those tears that stream?
A memory of a wilted flower, the sight of a grown child;
a butterfly unfolds its wings in flight.
The memories of long ago, of days gone by, a memory
of someone gone, of someone never to be seen,
brings back the tears.
I yearn for some familiar sign from the past to comfort, to reassure.
The eyes fill up with tears and they just stream—
the tears, those streaming tears—
for fear of the unknown that the future holds,
for fear of all rejections,
the tears, the tears just stream.
Should I hide? Should I depart from all my feelings?
How can I face each day of failure and rejection?
Don't ask me why the tears—
the tears just stream.
I cannot face each day for nothing has been left unturned or unspoken or undisclosed.
My life became an open book, a story without a pretty or a happy ending.
Those tears just stream.
The tears don't ease the pain or all the disappointments
but they still stream and stream,
those tears, those painful tears,
for fear of all that just awaits us,
those tears that stream and stream and stream.

November 3, 1995

Four Yellow Beeswax Candles

On a cold Sunday walking to the highway on a date
to meet a friend for lunch before my trip,
as I passed the church, I went inside while the Mass was on.
Into the vestibule I entered; the inner doors were closed.
Not wanting to get high on incense and the sound
as I bowed to mother goddess and her child in arms,
I did not kiss her in respect as all do and cross myself.
I bought four candles, yellow in their color and of beeswax.
Light a candle for my grandfather to set him free from sin.
Light another for my grandmother that I have never known
to take the pain from her for her life so short and painful death.
Then I light another for another grandfather who I knew so well
to set his soul up high with nature that he acknowledged toward his end.
One more candle I hold in my hand, thinking of love so gentle.
I have said a prayer in my heart to her not once but many times over.
This is for you, dear Grandmother, for your goodness and devotion,
so that your joy may live forever in the hearts of all you touched.
May your soul be reborn now and may you receive all the goodness that you gave.
I light that fourth last yellow beeswax candle and it goes aflame
glanced at all the flames that flicker and dance in darkness,
and I thought, *my dear departed, dance, sweet souls, dance once more.*

Peonies

My mother planted white peonies.
She abandoned them a long time ago.
They grow without attention;
They grow all on their own.
The white peony flower is so lovely,
it is so pure and white,
the scent intoxicating in the evening.
For such a graceful pure white flower
It's graceful poison to give around.
It can cure and it can kill.
What a strange and beautiful flower.

Baptism of my Granddaughter

My granddaughter was going to be baptized.
Her mother wanted that she should be like father.
I said since you are the mother you will teach her.

The relatives made her two sets of outfits,
spiritual pantaloons and dress in white and yellow.
We came to church; the priest was black Irish

All dressed in white like a druid's priest, black shoes.
He said *please gather all around the white marble altar
and hold each other's hands.* I was dressed in pink and white.

I bought a wedding ring of platinum and wheat that I put on.
I liked that priest I said, I'll marry him and thought of that.
Then he said some prayers or something like that.

He said *take all those clothes off the little one.*
He lifted little Christmas in Slavic and dunked in the pool.
He took her out and I thought *now she is a fish.*

A little ambrosial fish she now became,
A golden fish she is now, not with yellow pantaloons.
My marriage to the priest did not last a day.

I Cry in Silence

My mind is crying, my mood is black
I am lamenting over art, over what I cannot do
My breast is heavy, my emotions are aflame
My mind not at ease, it's overactive with a thought.
What holds me back, I do not know, or why
the easel stands, the canvas on, the painting still unfinished.
I cannot touch it or approach it, just look at it with desperation.
Six months have past and I'm still not finished.
So simple, so unpretentious and uncomplicated,
but I cannot approach it, cannot pick up a brush.
I look and heaviness of mind overtakes me once again.
I'm quiet, not one outburst and no protest; I have to finish it.
But how? My mind is numb, my mood is dark and low.
I cry inside, I scream in silence for some help
but no one hears me, no one is in sight but I alone.
I am alone; my mind is a scramble with emotions.
How long 'is it going to last this time—a day, a week, a month?
'I'm at a loss; there is no one, I'm alone with all my pain and agony.
I cry inside for help, for comfort and understanding, or some inspiration.

June 20, 2007

I Hear Voices in Silence

Voices out from nowhere, silent voices
Voices everywhere aware or unaware
Voices, voices, voices—loving voices, caring voices
Voices that make you feel so good
Voices telling you a thing or two
No arguing with voices, just conversing with the voices
They will tell you what to purchase, whom to give it to
Voices, telepathic voices—that's how it seems
But it's only voices, your own voices from your inner being that you hear
It will give you names
It will give you an address to deliver what you had painted
All you do is listen to the voices, and get astonished at the accuracy of names that you never heard of
And you deliver and it's real
Voices, voices, voices that don't argue nor insult
Voices that love you and elate you and admire you
Voices, voices, silent voices
You feel good, you feel great, you create, and you paint
You love; you fall in love with the voices that seem to come like telepathic voices
The voices seem to come from people; many different people
People whom you start to care for, people who exist
Voices, voices, they sound just like those people whom you see each day
And you believe the voices that deceive you, because you find out
They are not telepathic voices, but your inner voices that make you ill, that make you sick
Instead the loving feeling, instead the caring feeling, instead your elated feeling
Or your talent all becoming one foe
You created paintings; you wonder how you got the right name of a person
Whom you never met before to give it as a gift
You keep wondering if it's just a coincidence or some sort telepathic voices that told you
And you wonder for the rest of your existence
I never heard the names or knew the person, and yet the voices gave their names and they existed
You don't want the feeling to disappear, but you get tired of the voices
Tiresome voices when you want to sleep, but the voices still converse with you
They keep talking, and conversing voices, voices, voices
You feel so good all over, you're so happy and so high that you don't mind the voices;
Most seductive voices
You don't want the feeling to go away
It's your secret of the voices, as you call them,
Telepathic voices, silent voices, most seductive voices

Union Square Triangular Garden

Next to Union Square Park there is a small garden to the side. It is triangular in shape beside the station and the park. The fence is nicely made and encloses all around. The flowers are abloom; the green is sprawling on. There are some roses in bloom that are native to the country. They are growing in abundance on the beaches in the north. A tree stands at one end by the sidewalk all stretched out. It spreads its branches to all sides to cast some shade for passersby. No one stops to look or glance at this little haven by the park and at the other end there is a square stone with a bronze plaque. Atop that stone, cast in bronze, stands, humbly, barefooted Gandhi.

Three-year-old Remembrance of a Round House

I was stood in the corner quite often, my friends,
a punishment quite severe to my mind.
It always seemed for some reason unknown.
In a corner facing nowhere, in a corner,
I say, where two walls meet, a triangle to form.
I would stamp my small foot and scream,
In defiance I'd scream, *The corner's not mine, not mine!*
In defiance at the top of my lungs, I'd scream.
A round house is mine; a round house is my house.
When I' grow up 'I'll build a round house with no corners.
That is my house, round, with no corners at all
so no one will stand me in corners anymore.
Round house is the house that I want.
Round house I will have of my own.
A child I was; blue were my clothes, brown shoes on my feet.
Plaid was the woolen blanker that dragged from my shoulder.
To the floor it was dragging like some heavenly veil.
Round house is the house that I want.
Round house I will have of my own, of my own.
My mother, poor soul, never knew what to do.
A slap on my bottom would come like a bolt—
no tears when it came, no tears in defiance,
just screams of my house that is round.
Now, corners I have everywhere in my house,
more corners than house.

Love Abounds

O love, O love, O love—where has love gone?
Not far beyond my reach, if only I had wanted it,
love all around from left to right,
from head to toe if all you know.
It all abounds everywhere you go.
Look to your right, look to your left,
and all you see is a bright light that shines.
It shines like love that glows and glows
from years ago till now I know.
It was nearby, the love I knew,
The love I wonted all along.

O love, O love, O love, the love I longed for
like a candle flame aglow, like fire that is pure and warm.
It was nearby, the love I knew, the love I looked for, the love I could not see.
'It's right beside me; 'it's right by me,
the love I long for, the love I look for,
the love I could not give.
'I'll give it now if only I knew how,
the love that no one reached, you could reach now.
It all abounds with love around.
Like bright stars at night amidst dark blue skies,
above it twinkles and it plays its playful play.
It shines and it sings its serenade above.

O love, O love, O love, where has love gone?
Not far beyond my reach if only I will reach.
Not far beyond my touch if only I will touch.
Like candle flames aglow, like fire pure and warm,
love is all around us from left to right.
It's all around us from above so bright,
like sunshine in the midst of day,
It shines with its rays.
O love, O love, O love, where has love gone away?

June 23,1997
Beth Israel Hospital

The Mind Fixer

In limbo in a black hole I was.
Infinity was my prescription.
Black hole was my home and my life,
darkness of minds of others to know me.

Refusal of faith so quaint and unfair,
the visions, the sounds that all were in my mind
exploding in space in my mind on earth—
faces names reasons unknown to me or anyone else.

Appear disappear reappear to sadden and torment me,
inspired rebuffed and accused—
the cause and the doing is yours
That has dissented upon the home of my own.

A child cries when I do from despair
and then he was chosen by me on my own.
Confusion was then, and some disarray—
eager with blame toward me by my own.

He decided to sort all affairs one by one.
Order he brought; understanding he gave.
Time passed from days to months.
He kept healing the mind and thoughts.

Friendship he brought: understanding, compassion,
a smile to smile with each day that arrived,
to see the sun rise and to see the sun set,
to look up at the dark blue skies with wonder

At the moon at the stars that sit so high above all—
to feel love without madness of mind,
to think gentle thought of creations in mind—
A friend he became of my mind and soul.

The one who had given me life of my own,
he is my mind fixer first and most of all.
He sits facing me and I sit facing him;
a horizontal line is not crossed in between, and he heals.

In gratitude to my psychiatrist, Dr. David Roane.

Baptism of my Grandson

My grandson's baptism was very elaborate.
A Franciscan friar presided over it.
The godparents held candles; prayers were said.
A Mass was held on that day in his honor.
He was undressed, held to be dunked into the water,
but the friar held him in his arms,
then lowered him toward the water, not a touch,
then raised him up high to the sky.
I don't think that he is ambrosial fish.
I think he is a night—the moon the stars and the comet,
all in a pretty silver frame, little night he is.

Stained Soul

I have a dark secret to tell.
I'm no longer divided in three.
My circle divided in four for so long.

Once I had a small prince on the way
from the serpent with wings in the green.
Believed he did not and when he did

He wanted to fix it his way
but some one else intervened and caught on to him.
They killed my little prince in my ignorant way

My soul was stained by them until today.
My circle of fire divided by three was no more.
I'm earth that you walk on I'm four quarters inside.

I'm earth that you sow barley, corn, and wheat.
Before I left to come here, I saw him once more.
I spat in his face and walked all the way home.

In a Hospital

In a hospital alone I lay—
a gloomy room it is.
Lonely and abandoned, not the first time,
put away like luggage that's not used,
put by force by son and husband,
A way away as far as they can.

Not an answer to my question,
not a kind word to me.
Take away the freedom of,
put away the key and all,
all around making with a smile,
all around happy be because of me.

Put her out to pasture in a cell,
put her out of misery.
In a gloomy room we place her,
in a gloomy home of sick.
Illness she has none,
but out of the way she must be.

They insist upon an illness.
They insist upon a madness of the mind.
Who and way I cannot decipher
but one thing is clear to me—
out of the way they want me to be,
into a house of misery they put me.

Into a cell of darkness and indifference,
that is were I'm placed to be.
As I sit and glance from window
all I see is wall and skies of blue.
No one truly cares for my existence.
No one knows the misery that's mine.

Alone, alone with no one to insist well for me,
no one to hope for to see or hear,
no sadness or contentment in my heart,
just the knowledge how it all will be
into a cell of one that is doomed to be,
into that cell one more time you will be.

Someone's Pain I Felt

At 3:00 AM last morning
in anguish I woke up.
To sleep I was not able—
someone somewhere was in pain.

In pain of longing for some love,
my heart, my soul went out to the one.
The pain I felt was quite intense.
My love went out to reach that soul.

That soul of longing and of pain,
I take your pain away I said,
Embrace you in my arms with love.
The agony you feel is mine.

Sleep, love, sleep, love, may peace be yours.
The calmness of the universe upon you.
I reach for you with love and care.
Sleep, love, sleep, love, in my care tonight.

And all the pain I will receive.
Tear-streamed emotions overtaking sleep,
I felt the pain of longing for some love,
for care, for touch, desires, longing.

I cried in silence for that one unknown,
and the peace regained itself.
The course of morning sleep appeared.
The body ached with some desire.

The tears had stopped peace, peace.
All passed somehow unknown.
At 3:00 AM last morning in stillness
I felt you and I felt your pain.

So deep and so profound into my soul,
I do not want you hurting in the night.
I do not know you in the morning—
in some distant place you are.

Your pain and longing is all I feel.
Who are you and where? Please answer
so I can take your pain away
and I will give you peaceful sleep

Red

Red is the color of passion, a color of fire inside me,
passion beyond control, a passion of insanity,
out ragged and ragged to all surroundings,
red light, red district, red hair of some special tribes,
red velvet, red ruby, red apples, red, red, red—

All so enticing, all so inviting to touch and to feel.
The fire is burning inside me and wanting to burst.
Sparks are afloat—my soul rises up—I'm floating above fire.
The serpent on my finger has red ruby eyes to hypnotize.
He is coiled and round and sits quite nice in his place.

Red raspberries, red strawberries, oh, what a delight!
But rage overtakes me—the seeds all got stuck.
The strawberries made me so itchy that I must scratch.
Red are my arms from scratching so hard.
My nails on my toes were painted bright red to seduce.

Pretty red skies at sunset sometimes, but beware of the promise.
The promise is fateful to red, and the next day the wind blows.
My blood is red in my veins and it's salty and thick.
Sometimes I dribble it on white paper to see life.
Red for a planet beyond reach and so far to the sight.

A wedding dress of red silk made for a bride far away,
A red linen shroud for my burial will be nice.
Lay me on red stones and cover me with red earth tonight.
Do not place red roses—they are for lovers alone, not for a dead bride,
Nor red carnations—they belong to señoritas that dance.

If you want to remember me, plant a redwood and leave it to thrive.
Good-bye, my dear friends, adieu and farewell to you all.
I send you a kiss from my painted red lips, and a wave of my hand
with my fingernails painted red to match my toenails,
I shall seduce you, all wrapped up in red as I'm laid in my grave.

Pelentown Cemetery

I often pass by Pelentown cemetery ground
by my brother's country house.

The birch trees are the only trees around.
It's quiet, it's peaceful at that ground.

Some stones are ancient and some new.
I never see the mourners bound.

Some have flags, some have flowers,
but nowhere else are the birch trees to be found.

Sometimes I pass toward the evening hour.
The last sunrays shine their golden rays around.

I want to buy a piece of ground
on this tiny hill that they call Pelentown cemetery ground

Next to a field of tall grass that so abounds,
surrounded by hemlock trees all around

With the birch trees that are nowhere else to be found.
What a resting place I've found.

Innocence Lost

Young, innocent, naïve I was, and full of life.
From school I walked one day past iron gates.
Across the street was a wall and I have sat

Staring at the soldier in the red beret there.
I stared and stared at him for so long that he crossed the road.
"Little girl," he said to me, "what is your name? Please tell."

At first with indignation I replied, *not little any more*
My name is Christmas. "You want a ride back home?"
I hopped into the jeep next to the flying serpent in green.

Home he brought me and asked to see me late at night.
At evening hour late that day, I sneaked outside alone.
He drove up high into the mountain where the pines grow.

We sat on pine needles beneath the darkened skies.
He asked me, "Am I the first?" and I replied *O, no, dear sir.*
Grown up I wanted to be; I did not understand.

He took me in his arms so close and so dear
and showered me with his kisses and love
and I saw with closed eyes the stars and the skies.

The last time I saw him we sat on a bench in a park.
Before coming here he asked, "Why did you lie?"
I left him puzzled till today why I said he was not the first.

Little Green Grass

After all that had settled with my shambled life at the store, little green brown green from the bugs reappeared. It started to tell and to whisper to me and to send me on my way. Into every direction it sent me and never stopped the whisper, my mind aflame, no sleep in my frame, just greasy whispers. All sorts of questions about me—go here, go there, give this to that one, give this to another, and buy some more. There was no resistance from fatigue and no real calling.
I gave my presents and all precise things to others under instructions. That grass, greenish brown, should be sacrificed in the bugs and drowned.

For several years it tormented me. It wanted me to be a white bird, to be a white bird that flutters its wings in despair. Your sister is the white one, the one I kept meeting on platforms of trains, just because I wore white woolen trousers and white coat from a lamb. My beret was white, too, with my crest embroidered on. No fluttering bird was, I no fluttering dove I am.
My coat of arms will prove it. I have several of them—black eagle with a sword in one claw, a ball with a cross in the other, and a lance that killed a dragon, too, in my name, and a shield with a wave above a coronet and a ball with a cross, some olive branches and one fleur-de-lis.

I am not your sister or your fluttering dove from a church. I fence like a soldier. I fence with a glove and a sword.

Memories of the Poet I Met

It was a cold blue-sky day on Ellis Island.
I sat behind a desk of sorts out there by myself, all alone,
staring at the people passing by.
I had to sell some spaces on the memorial wall, I'm told.

St Patrick's Day was approaching next day, and a parade, too,
and I dressed in green ahead to welcome Celtic blood, I thought.
In green I sit to prove the fact to all the passersby that day.
I sit awaiting clientele to come and talk that day.

A genteel man from far away with open coat approached.
He came to me to say hello, red folder under arm.
Irish was he, from far away he came to write a poem, he said.
He asked me for my name and if Irish I am.

"Why, my dear lady, you are in green," he said.
"Irish you must be, just like I am, blue eyes like mine, it must be so."
The smile on his face had broadened with contentment; so gentle was he,
So dignified he looked in woolen navy blue.

He dashed away on a tour of Ellis Island but he said he will write too.
Poet he is that dashes away with his coat flung open and swinging.
His eyes were sky blue, his smile so gentle and true,
I wondered if really he'd write in the future from Ireland to me.

To Australia, he said, he is dashing away for a while.
"You will hear from me, my dear lady," he said and left with a smile.
Some months had passed by and I heard not a word.
I took matters my way with that poet I met.

I send him some greetings and tidings from me on my own.
I thought a poet he is, I must keep him for me.
I'm possessive and greedy when it comes to such things.
I thought he had found me in the crowd.

A poet he is, that's all I could think, a poet, a poet and more,
Irish poet, no more or no less, how lucky I am that he ran into me.
How lucky I was that he thought Irish I was with that sweater of mine,
Green, as green as the apples I love, so Irish, that green like the grass.

Dedicated to my Father Whom I Did Not Know

I had no father but an accidental father,
not by choice but by remorse.

I thought of a father far away,
a father that was taken by some fate unseen.

I give my blessing to that father that I long to know,
so far away and quite unknown.

I wrote some letters of my longing for you, Father,
only to reflect my love and sorrow for a father.

Gray were some days without a father.
Tears streamed on gray days of thoughts about you, Father.

Joy was to know that you were alive.
Sorrow was abound without you, Father.

I did not know you, O dear, dearest Father.
Be happy that we all have found each other.

Be happy that that you are a father.
Love abounds for you, my Father.

A babe was I then and old I am now.
I reach to you with love, my dear Father.

I lay a path of rose petals in your way,
A life beyond unknown love and peace, dear Father.

Known or unknown, found or unfound,
you shall always be my dearest and well loved father.

Berlin Wall

If you are ever going to be in Berlin,
look at the pictures on the wall
and you will see something that few know:
How the black prince of darkness
carries the red one in his arms in flames.

And next to it you will see her face in red.
I wanted to enlarge it but he started to scream.
He grabbed me and started to choke me.
I slowly pulled out a knife and he dropped me,
and I hadn't even had painted the scene.

But I guess he remembers from before,
how the fireman called to me, "Hey, Red,"
and he doesn't like it at all.
A violent nature he has, as you see,
but no one believes me somehow.

He really doesn't know much about certain things
and that's how I like it to be.
He praises me to others as if I were a saint.
Sometimes I think that he mistakes me
for someone that once he had known.

It's not once I have said that flames are my passion.
The dark in my life is a passion.
I shall follow it to the end of the world
and no one can stop me from being as I am,
Not even he, with a knife in his hand.

White Roses in a Silver Vase

Just memories of roses, white and pure,
three green orchids and green berries.
All were set in silver pretty vase,
a small bouquet so precious and so dear,
so white and pure like bride's flowers.
O, who had sent so precious a gift to me?
O, who was dear and kind to me I do not know.
I cared for them for weeks to come with love,
looking at them with wonder and surprise.
O, who has sent such wonder and delight?
O, who was kind thoughtful and so loving?
A small white bouquet of roses in a silver vase,
so many, so late for a white bouquet of roses.
Such wonder in my heart: Who sent the roses?
I kept the silver vase for lilies white and yellow roses.
O, how wonderful was the bouquet of white roses.
a gift of love and mystery unknown about the white roses.

Dear Friends

My love and devotion to both of my friends,
to her and to him with the children on hand,
the children that came to my house every morning,
the girls that I loved each in different ways,
One quiet, so lonesome she seemed in the mornings,
And the other so lively and playful with my son.
Each one got a place in my heart like my own.
I loved them so dearly and still love them both.
Grown up they are now, and gone on their own.
I think with small wonder how beautiful the mornings were,
the sound of laughter, the giggles and noise.
How blest all that have children on hand!
I held their small hands as I put them on the bus.
My son was so happy, so mischievous and playful.
O, how lovely and blessed were those days in my life!
My older was gone early each morning to school.
O, how I loved them all, and still do to this day.

Enchanted

The enchanter was enchanted by no means of knowing. I was enchanted by your kind heart and mind, by your eyes as black as coal. Your burning eyes of coal are full of knowledge, of forbidden passion, too. Gentle smile, gentle manner, and at times, so stern, like a godly man you are. Overwhelmed with so many thoughts, overburdened with so many burdens of the spirit and the mind, you have enchanted me along the way.

How strange; I was supposed to be the one, I thought, that I alone enchanted somehow. The victims of my soul are captives of my spirit; they were always my own. But you, my dearest, have enchanted me instead, the gentle man you are. Those burning eyes of coal, the smile that I envision every night, somehow the look, the eyes that look into my eyes with genteel thoughts of telling of some things of wonder and delight, of mind, spirit, and the soul.

I am enchanted to a fright of all that I envision in my dreams tonight. O, dearest love, enchanter of my soul, my mind, my spirit is imprisoned by a thought. You are enchanting me each night, with the onset of stars in the dark blue skies. The gentle breeze that touches me tonight caresses me as if it were you. I was supposed to be the one who set the spells of mood upon the man of my choice. I have touched you, but you have touched my life with care and gentle wonder. You have enchanted me with love and song and dance upon my moods.

I wore a garland of fresh flowers upon my head tonight and danced under the moon to music of slow flutes and gentle voices praising you at night beneath the stars. I am enchanted in my secret garden, beneath the stars and scented air of night I hug you and I thank you for being who you are, enchanter of my spirited heart. I thank you for the favor you have done for me, that you are the one who enchanted me.

Winter of 1999

Dedicated to George Finocchiaro

For Fathers Day

Arise, fair knight, for the occasion.
The night is young,
the moon is bright,
the stars are golden in their color,
and the skies are free of clouds.
Be proud of being a father.
Be glad for sons for lasting name.
Let's celebrate tonight in your honor,
let's raise a glass to your desire
with all our love from sons
offspring's and a wife.
I say rise up, fair knight,
and I salute you for existing on this earth.
Let's celebrate for being and existing,
let's give thanks for living.
I knight you, my fair friend, for all devotion.
Let's celebrate till sunrise.

April 1999

Farwell to Bridget

Farewell, dear Bridget,
Farewell St. Bridget.
Say farewell to the Mark,
To the laughter and the tears,

To the happy moments and sad ones,
Farewell to the good and the bad.
Meet your future and all the moments of fear or indecision,
And moments of knowledge and strong will.

Embrace your new life, your sunny new path,
Embrace the freedom like sunshine in the sky.
I bid you farewell and may luck go with you.
I bid you a path strewn with happiness too.

May all your days be sunshine, the moon and stars,
May you never fear, cry, or retreat from your sun or your stars,
May happiness follow every step of the way,
May your future hold as bright as a basket of St. Bridget.

May your life be as colorful as those flowers.
I shall always remember you as you are.
My fondness of you shall never diminish.

May 15, 1999

I Am a Russ

Many times I thought that in my past I was the Empress Tatuzhashy,
The proud, the powerful, the mean, the cruel,
And then one day I fell in love with Celtic pride.
This time I thought that in the past I was a Celtic queen.
I went to battle and fought till death by side of naked men,
All dressed in velvet and green silk, red hair blowing in the wind.
And then I thought again, no, maybe an Indian princess,
Dressed in all her fineries and bejeweled,
Stood on pyres beside her husband who was laid in death.
They poured the butter and put the torch to consume by fire.
That was the custom and the duty of a wife—to join him in flight.
And then it dawned on me one day like lightning, I'm the past of Russ.
I was sacrificed to heavens and the land and sun.
I walked among the light ones in furs and silk and fine linens.
All were embroidered with gold and studded with precious stones,
But some unfortunate and unpredictable event came to be.
The Russ tribe gathered and the priest in white announced,
We need to sacrifice a maiden from the higher up.
They showed me to the crowds of tribal Russ with pride,
This is our holy maiden who will bring the peace
They laid me on the wooden altar and the priest raised the dagger.
I lay there without motion or emotions or any fright.
Some people screamed and some cried some yelled stop,
But he with all of his persistence with a chant has stabbed me in the heart.
You see, I do remember of my past life well.
I was a Russ and still am now in this life, too.

June 9, 1999

Hydrangea Bush

In the corner that is fenced
stands a round hydrangea bush.
It used to flower into blue color,
then it changed to purple.

Now it blooms pink and lavender.
It is a lovely, lush hydrangea full of buds.
The bush is round, the leaves are green.
I wait for it to flower.

But the bush has enemies abounding.
As people pass, they tear the flower
until no flower's left at all.
The bush stands torn here and there.

It must be trimmed each day of the lost flowers.
The bush is round, the leaves are green,
But naked of any other color.
I wait for the hydrangea bush to flower.

July 5, 1999

The Birth of Vlademar

To welcome Vlademar, the sky thundered with delight.
The stars sparkled and danced all night in the dark sky.
Among the floating planets far above, the angels sang of praise.
The day arrived—the sun spread its rays and shone like gold.
The birds sung their song of happiness to him alone—
Happiness, delight of life, position, station—all will be your right.
The church rung the bells to welcome you today.
Vlademar the child has arrived to his father's delight.
Mother's tears flooded rivers to overflow with joy and happiness.
Grandmother and grandfather puffed their chests with pride.
Great grandmother was the most full of happiness delight and pride.
The sister just became an aunt with curiosity and genteel fright.
We raise a toast to Vlademar, to health, no speeches, please, tonight.
Enjoy, dance, eat, be merry now Vlademar is one of us.
We raise another toast long life, to the lineage of a family with dignity and pride.

Sept 3, 1999
Dedicated to my cousin Lydia's great grandson

My Anger Directed at You

Suffer your own plight with your age.
Suffer your own pain as you go,
like you made me suffer alone,
like I suffered from what you have done me.

Suffer the pain and the longing.
Suffer the longing for child unknown.
Suffer your plight, suffer with pain.
Let your mind be all so unrested.

Let your thoughts wander some more.
If you ever will see me,
contempt is in my heart for your doing.
Suffer alone in agony and pain

Like you made me suffer for years.
Unrest is your medicine now for the years,
For the sacrifice that I made in your name.
Suffer, my love, suffer no end.

Pain of Spirit and Soul

Abused and hurt you left me to be
accused for wrong lies you told.
The music stopped and you abandoned me.
The sun set deep into the sea.
The skies darkened with no moon.
The stars have not shone for me at all.
You hurt my spirit and my soul.
You sank my life from light to dark.
O, where you took my life and dignity,
you have abused my mind and my flesh.
How many lies you told to save your soul!
O, how I loved you then to let you go!
They told me that your future would be so great;
I wonder now how great your future is.
That I have let you go, I gave you freedom,
freedom that you wanted from your lies.
O, how you hurt me, love, I cannot tell.
I paint sunsets all over to forget the pain.
I once was on a ship at sea and watched the sun,
the wonder and the beauty as it spread its rays.
The sun is disappearing with your name at sea.
I watched the sun at sea for weeks to come.
No pain was there, no pain at all,
until I watched the sun with you somewhere.
I do not remember being against the sinking sun.
The pain is great, the memory is almost none.
Shock treatments have erased the visions
but the pain is still inside my mind and soul.
Sunset's memories are a wonderful calm.
Just paint it all—the sea, the water, and the ships,
the ships that come and go somewhere.
Paint mingles with love on canvas with feelings.
Each stroke of the paint tells of my feeling.
O, love, why did you hurt me so much in this life?
My circle is ending with pain in my mind, my spirit, and my soul.

Prince of Darkness

He is my prince of darkness
and I'm his shining star.
The stars shine at night
with the onset of midnight,
with the stars flickering
in the rose scent of the night,
the smell of the snow not too far,
the scent of the pine quite near.
The tides rise, the moon shines—
it all casts magic on earth.
The lovers dance in each other arms.
The song is sung in praise to all.
The prince is mine alone.
This is my message to all.

January 3, 2000

China

I left you in a hurry, my homeland.
On a long train ride I was put.
I'm told, not mine, you are dear land.
O, I loved you, China, you were my home,
from long ago you were.
Singing I did in the train all the way
south from my land to Hong Kong
and out of my land that was no more.
Today I returned—your arms received me once more.
I was born, like you in that land of magic.
China, I still love you so.

Bali

I lay outside on the divan, resting on the cushions,
watching the lighting and the rain all night till dawn.
The waves of sliver color in the distance glared
against the dark dark skies with thunder in the air.

My twenty hours of wonder and amazement are upon me,
and the amazing beauty of Bali engraved in my soul.
The incense was light each day; with dusk the smell was in the air,
The fruit replenished in the middle of the table in a dish with a cover.

Silky cushions to recline on the divan in leisure,
the greenery in that small garden with a cricket on a statue,
an Eden in Bali, a paradise, a small private garden with a view.
It cannot be described in words alone—one must experience it.

Beyond words or descriptions, it was not illusion or delusion.
It was real—it's there still—the frangipane trees,
the tub of cool water full of rose petals and frangipane flowers
to sink in for one's pleasure and to bathe and be born anew.

That is a small description of Bali and its paradise,
The paradise that I had found, that I have read about.
At night the scent from white frangipane flowers,
the warm walks along the ways at moonlight every night.

A paradise at the other corner of the earth,
a paradise only for the tourist and the rich.
The paradise in the villas that are so private and so guarded,
no paradise for natives or the artist.

No money, no paradise of luxury or comfort,
just nature, beaches, streets, heat, and dust,
narrow streets, dusty roads, cemetery behind closed fences,
but all in all I loved it all—the sun, the heat, and the Buddhist ways.

January–February 2000

Paradise Found and Lost

I lay beneath the dark starry skies in the Isle of Bali
in comfort of the princes that once were.
The thunder echoes from far away across the sea.
Lightning strikes nearby into the silver waves.

I lay in leisure and in comfort against silk cushions.
The feel of silk and luxury are mine tonight.
Oh, how wonderful the lush green garden and the pool!
Oh, how blessed I am tonight to witness nature's wonders.

The scent of frangipani in bloom is strong all over
and the sea water rushes onto the shore.
Volcanic stones are wet with rushing water and the foam.
I hear the sound of the water from the sea waves.

The skies are lit by lightning; some flickering stars remain.
The moon is hiding behind the clouds it's dark, it's silver light.
Love, O, love, I think of you not once but thrice each night.
I lost you to someone somewhere, I do not know to whom,

And gained another that is not beside me any longer.
I witness all the wonder that surrounds me alone—
sweet air and warm nights, the beauty that surrounds me.
I thought of paradise, I dreamt of it, I read of it, and then I found it here.

Paradise, discovered by the warmth and the scented air,
green lush mountains, sun, sand, and sea, a misty rain—
the night itself could be sweet haven of paradise itself
in the arms of some beloved from far away under the skies.

I own illusions and some disillusions of some thoughts,
those thoughts and things are not beside me; they are lost in time,
lost somewhere to someone else, some other paradise,
somewhere at night that has another love and scent of flower.

Another man and dark starry sky with thunder in the air,
with silver sea reflection of the moon upon it, and misty rain—
I lost my paradise to someone else somewhere at night,
But to whom I do not know. Warm rain caresses me right now

February 2000

Wondrous Wonder in My Life

I wonder sometimes of my pretty little girl.
Is she a princes or a queen to be?
Does she love or does someone loves her like I do?

I wonder is her hair still black like his used to be?
O, wonders wondrous wonder, for I'll be
just like I looked in the crowds and the trains.

For her father, that is like she was then—
never ran into either one, not him or her,
and if I did, so what would I say to him or to her?

Would I cry or would I walk jut quietly away?
A silent person I have became with my age.
No malice I ever held for anyone on this earth.

No hate in my heart or my mind for him,
but there is this longing to know what he thinks.
Did he ever liked me? Was I pleasing to him?

Was I just a sacrifice in his life?
But why give me these feelings now?
I was in my youth quite nice looking.

But I became with age and my illness changed.
Silent I became, no temper any longer to flame.
I wish both of you goodwill with my wandering love.

September 2000

Lamenting

In blood, I wrote your name not once
with love and memories of sadness,
with pain and suffering was it, too, for me.
You were the one the only one I truly loved.
Not once I thought of you, each day gone by.
How beautiful were you as I remember you from youth—
your face, your hands, your voice—I heard it as a melody
of tender love and care for me when I was small.
I marched with you unspoken miles in the wars.
I held your hand to guide me into safety then.
How much I loved you then, how mach I love you now!
O, dearest dear love of youth gone by and through,
Through pain and miseries gone by and by
we marched together when I grew up with you.
You are the angel of my thoughts inspired,
you are the angel that had kissed me first.
How I adored you and still adore you now.
I do not see you anymore as I had seen you then.
O, love, blind I have become to please someone
I crucified and nailed to unknown wood.
Not once they nailed me because of loving you.
My darkest friend, the darkest angel that you are,
I gave you all I had from youth till now
with love and no regrets on my part.
If ever you will need my help, it's yours, o, love,
dark, dark most beautiful and dearest angel that you are.

July 26, 2000

Lamenting Two

O, dearest, dearest on this earth you are!
O, precious more than gold and silver be!
I sing to you my melody of love and praise.
I sing out loud that all may hear the melody,
the lyrics of this song I wrote for thee
to praise thee and caress thee with my words.
I raise a crystal glass of wine to you
and sing an ode of love from past till now,
of struggles and of happy moments we had,
of disagreements and of all arguments we had.
Please listen to my song I sing to thee of love.
I thank you for all the flowers that you sent.
I thank for all the patience that you have with me.
Uneasy is my spirit and my soul, you know,
not easy is it to be with me—you know it, too.
We struggled through, and through each day we came,
but I have never stopped my love for you.

You Could Have Been My Sunshine

You could have been my sunshine
But instead I gave you up.
Tears and despair fill up my heart.

Pain and agony does overcome me.
Without direction and advice, I gave you up.
All I could think was to give you a better life.

So many times I wonder where you are.
My heart is aching just to know you.
At times, I think how I should have done it.

But youth was in the my way, my dearest.
I had no knowledge of the outcome,
of the pain and tears that come.

I had no knowledge of the longing for you, sunshine.
I do remember you and always will till death.
I reach to you with love and kindness and all hope.

Maybe someday we will reach for one another—
that is my hope, my love, I shall remember you forever.
There is no way that I'll forget you, sunshine.

April 6, 2001

The Love of Two Sons

Of two sons, both loving and both caring,
two sons are different in temperament and age
and yet so tender and so caring.
Both see the need to love and care.

There is no need to wonder why they are the way they are.
In youth they received their love and care
and as adults they give it back to me,
that gentle, tender love and caring.

All the love that in their hearts, it is for me,
and some of it for their family.
Of two sons, both loving and both caring,
there is no other joy in life than children.

Loving, gentle, caring children,
the two sons that I have and hold,
my love is strong for them as theirs for me,
I have found the time for them just like they find it for me.

April 2001

I am the Sun

I am the sun, the burning sun.
I give life to the forest and the earth.
The earth revolves around me in seasons.
I am the burning fire in the skies

I burn forest grass and homes.
I burn Celts with fire of the sun,
The Celts, the ones that worship fire and the sun.
I am the circle with a dot inside me.

I warm seasons and give light.
The god has placed me in the circle of the stones
to cast the sun upon the wood to flame,
to burn grass and burn forests.

I am no goddess but a flaming sun,
a flaming, burning, and exploding sun.
We worship fire, stones, and sun,
The fire from the sun that burns homes.

It makes charcoal that we bury in the walls.
I am the sun, the circle with the dot.
The Celts had worshiped it in ancient times
and still worship sun and fire.

The circle and the dot my symbol,
my signature upon this earth.
I am no love goddess of the Greeks of ancient times.
I am no Venus of long ago, but a circle and a dot.

August 2002

To my Beloved

I have professed my love for you in blood.
There is no one like you on earth.
You are the one the only one for me.
In all the darkness of the night I am with you,
in all the seasons come and past
there is no end or a beginning for my love for you.
I never met someone like you or never will.
My heart is yours just like my flesh.
You make me sing of endless songs.
You make me gaze at stars with wonder.
A prince you are of darkness and all wonder.
I'll spend my life with you to all eternity to come.
My love for you is overflowing
like the rivers in the forest,
Eternal love and so profound
that I'm yours for years on end.
I shall be humbled in your presence.
I shall be loving and adore you.
Remember this—there is no one like you for me,
My dearest, sweetest man of all,
no one evokes the love in me like you.

August 2002

Sun's Explosion

The mood is high, the mind is manic—
explosive energy is flowing in all directions.
Desire to paint overtakes me by and by.
Is there a canvas? Is there oil paint?

I put the canvas on the easel.
I take red paint, I'll make a statement
squeezing paint onto the palette
Now a brush, a round one—I swirl it in the paint.

Starting from the middle with the paint,
stretching outward red and bold—
now a bit of yellow in between—
colors mingle from the middle outward.

Colors stretching outward to the edge,
red and yellow—mostly red—all over.
Now excitement overtakes me and my mind.
It's exciting and it's pleasing to the senses.

I have covered every inch of canvas with the paint.
Such energy had flowed I did not stop
and I thought, with a step away from it,
I have created an abstract, a kaleidoscope in paint.

My mind eased, the energy subdued,
a great relief and pride has overtaken me.
I have achieved something beautiful without drawing—
my inner explosion of energy and imagination..

For Natasha

The birthdays come and go
but love for you remains
like flowers that are blooming in the spring,
like angels' songs at night.
The stars may shine bright for you,
the sun shall warm you up,
and the snow in winter bring you luck
as pure and shining white.
May all the love we have for you
just bring all warm wishes and good luck.
May life be kind to you and full of love.

November 27, 2002

Anger at Liars

I was taught not to lie, for I won't be punished for it
but the mate is one big liar that will not admit to it.
He wants to put it over me, in front of some to judge me harsh.
Oh, how I hate the thing he says, oh, how I despise that mood of his.
Superior he appears to some, to make me so inferior with his lying,
but I'm strong; and maybe stronger than he is,
I do hate liars, oh, how I do hate lies, I do hate lies.
I was thought not to lie, for I won't be punished for it.
I have no reasons for any lies; I'd rather tell of nothing at all than lie.
Omit the stories and the tales; omit what bothers me the most,
but by God I will not tell lies, by God I won't.
Oh, how I hate him telling lies, because I was thought not to lie,
for I won't be punished for them, I won't be punished.

November 27, 2002

Illusions and Disillusions

Illusions and disillusions, I wish that I remembered what you said to me. We stood so close and spoke so soft, with face to face so that almost I could touch you. I saw your features and they engraved in me, that morning tears were shed. I wish that I remembered what you said to me on that night that seems so long ago. Your presence every morning that I saw each day will not live my mind. So many loving thoughts that cross my mind each night, just sitting or just standing. Your image I see with my eyes open and I will kiss it, even now today. I took my black and hung it the closet, I asked you what you want to be. You wanted nothing, just like me, and in my dreams I could not see. But now that I'm far away from you, I see you with my dreamy eyes that close at night. I kiss you and I hug you, for what you taught to me. Not easy were my days but seeing you each day has eased the pain. Your presence calmed me no end. Each day I see you with my eyes closed tight, just like with my eyes open wide, I see your dark, dark eyes. I long to stand by you right now and to remember of what we spoke that night. The thought of you brings tears to me as I'm writing these few words. I think of you with warmest and most loving thoughts, to see you and your face facing mine.

I did not know your name when we last spoke, but I longed to know it the mornings after you had come, to face me so I could see your name. I have no memory for names at all, just faces that I see and long to know, but you engraved it in my mind, like magic of some sort, so I'll remember it. I am just an artist; no structure do I have. I float from day to day in struggle from canvas to a paper and a pen.

I wish you luck, I wish you the love that I know so well, that tears flow easy to my eyes as I raise a toast to you have a merry Christmas.

Good-bye, farewell, adieu. May all the love and wisdom follow you wherever you may go.

December 4, 2002

Inspiration from Someone's Love

The thought of you, my love, just makes me high and full of love.
A certain feeling of some longing to create overtakes my mind—
how you inspire me, my love, you'll never know.
I want to write, I want to paint, and all for you alone.

There is no one like you, my love, there is no one.
I see your image not once but twice and thrice.
If only I could give the world to you, I would.
I thank you for the way you are, I thank you most.

O, how I want to let you know how much you mean to me!
There is no one like you around, no one at all.
You have inspired me in the past; you do inspire now.
O, love, there is no one like you at all, nowhere.

To think of you, o, love, like in the garden of the night
among the blossoms of sweet flowers and get inspired,
or maybe disappear to where I'll think of love,
of love so deep and so profound that every time I am inspired.

Tears come to my eyes as I'm thinking of your image.
Where are you, love? Maybe you are nowhere near me.
I curl up in bed and say good night to you each night
and as the morning comes, I think of you, my love, sweet love.

December 2002

Unquiet Moments

I'm still in love with you, my moor, and you want to show your feelings,
and when I think of you, my heart's so glad and full of love.
If only you had known of my love for him, he would be glad.
There is no way of telling him of all the love I have for him.
I have no words that simple to describe it, or to tell someone.
My love is secret and unknown to him; it is so hidden you can't tell,
but when I think of him, my heart is sad and glad.
At times, I want to tell him, but I do not know if he will lend an ear
or what he'd say to me, if I was to tell the truth about my love.
My love is overflowing with the love for him unending,
and when I see his image or I see him in full life, I lose the courage.
Unquiet is my mind and unquiet are my thoughts of him.

I love him to no end to come, I love him with the heart that overflows.
Pleas tell me how to tell him or what to do; because I safer to no end.
Sometimes I think he knows of my love for him and pays no head to it.
It gives him pleasure to know I'm weak and fell for him completely.
My moor is tall and handsome, with the darkest eyes you ever saw,
dark hair and curls crowning his head to overflow.
I do not cry for him at night, not any more, but long for him to know.
Unquiet are my thoughts, and a heavy feeling overtakes my breast.
I long for him to know my feelings, but my moor is no magician.
If some day I have the courage I will summon it to me to tell him of my love
and then I'll suffer very little, because my moor does not belong to me,
But at least he'll know of my love for him that overflows and tears won't flow.

December 2002

Dearest of Them All

The dearest of them, the dearest of them all,
you stood me by, you healed my mind, so
O, how I love you so, no one will ever know.
You asked of nothing in return, just well for me.

I love you for what you are, for what you do to me.
There is no one like you in sight, there is no other.
You asked for nothing but just the truth of me.
Just when I'm high, to let you know of that.

And I that love it so you will not reveal it to anyone,
but you return me back to me as I am now.
I do not like that feeling, or that mood at all.
After awhile it all comes back to me, as if it never left my side.

There never were the lies or any of deceptions.
You only wanted best for me, to heal my mind
and yet, I keep hiding it from you.
I want to walk at night under the stars and think.

The mind is complex; the thoughts are strange at times
but when I see you, dearest, it all comes straight in line.
There is no one like you, my dearest, of them all.
The smile and the eyes that look to mine.

It's cold outside; the sun is spreading some rays right now.
I did not sleep last night; new room, no heat, tomorrow I shall see,
And when I face you, dearest, you heal my body and my mind.
There is no one like you to be found anywhere around.

December 3, 2002

Christmas 2002

Cheers, cheers, and cheers,
for Christ the child is born.
The star is guiding us to him,
the shepherds gathering around
to welcome him tonight like every year,
and we'll gather, all, to praise his name.
Peace, peace on earth to all
in prayers and in song, and bells will ring
for merry is the eve of Christmas like the day,
And soon New Year's will come with kings.
Cheers, cheers, cheers to all on the New Year.

December 22, 2002

Ray

I met someone so gay and full of life,
so understanding to know the end to come.
I wish that all his pain be gone,
just love and joy remaining.
I wish that all would understand the artist
so he could have the peace to paint the best,
and most of all I wish him love and joy.
May all his friends gather round him,
and may the New Year take the pain.
No disappointments for 2003, just greatest luck shall be,
but not for one New Year alone to come,
but for all the rest to follow, too.

Dec. 2002

Season's Greetings

Season's greetings and best wishes—
may it be the merriest of all the seasons,
full of snow and warmth inside your doors.
May it bring your wants and your desires,
all the love and glowing fire that you wish.
May your home be loving kind, may the love be full aglow.
There no other wishes from my heart but peace.
May you never know the unhappy moments that I know.
I hope the New Year bring you luck such as you have never known,
Luck that continues through and through forever more.
There are no more fond loving wishes then these are alone—
happy holiday season and happy New Year!

December 2002

Happy New Year

Happy New Year—the bells will ring,
the glass full of champagne will bubble
and rise for good cheer for dear friends,
for all that two thousand and three will bring.
We all will remember good in the past,
all will dance till dawn or morning to come.
The sunrays will spread their warm glow like fire
and once more the glass will fill to the brim
for health, for peace, and the New Year.
To welcome Christmas for what it really means,
I shall raise a glass to you all in good cheer

December 2002

Frustration

I walk toward the studio, open the door.
Boxes and boxes confront me.
I step for moment and think *where will I store it?*
Frustration confronts me all over again.

It's been now a month and I haven't moved anything.
Boom! I slam the door and out of the room,
back to kitchen I walk to pace and to think.
To the back stairs I'm marching to smoke.

Frustration, frustration, all over again,
day in and day out and no solution to be found.
Back a few steps from the back stairs to dining room.
Boxes on the floor and the paintings confront me.

I pace all over again. Where will I store everything?
I give up and back to kitchen I go, frustrated.
My mood is getting low—maybe I'm tired and need a rest.
To disarrayed living room I go to lay down on the couch.

Frustrated, depressed, and can't get a shut eye.
The mind is racing—maybe it will all fall into place,
from two floors into one somehow.
Frustrated, I can't lay still; I get up.

Back to the back stairs again for a smoke.
I want everything in its place; I want to paint.
No easel to put the canvas on; it was damaged in the fire.
Frustration, frustration, all over again.

2003

Dead Inside

I'm dead inside,
my imagination gone away somewhere.
I'm low and lonely and feel abandoned.
I yearn for excitement and adventure,
for someone's love that does not exist.
I cannot write or hear voices.
The end to all is nearby now.
I'm numb and dead inside,
But I try, O, how I try.
I'm surrounded by love but cannot see it.
All is dull and pale, all I see is black.
My creativity is gone aflame
O, but I try, O, how I try.
My mind is quiet now, there are no voices,
there are no recollections to be told,
there are no stories to write down.
All is calm in my mind now
but I still yearn and long
for the times past that were so active.
I'm dead inside, I'm dead inside
I cannot write, O, but I try.

Black Hole

Everything an effort, no peaks at all, just vales and black holes, black holes.
Getting up from bed is an effort, and to shower, too. To get outside is frightening; nothing to do.

Black hole, black hole, why have you descended, why have you descended upon my life once more?
I do not want to live the way I am now—I want to live in sunny warmer weather now.

The mind is just not moving without the peaks. The highs that so I do miss are gone without return. I do not know what to do. The life I live is desolate. Black hole, please go away, please go away.

Frustration and an effort at everything I do.
To eat it is an effort, to clean I cannot do.
Just vales at some points, but mostly just black holes.
Please leave me to one more cigarette to ease the pain.

Black holes, black holes, please leave me to sunshine. Give back my peaks, my highs and laughter.
Please leave me now to be what I was once—creative and inspired without black holes.

May 22, 2003

Summer's Love

Two lovers in each other's arms by the ocean
Summer breeze caress them with love
The skies are studded with the stars, the moon is new
Whispers, whispers of some love between them
Blue and warm are the waters of the ocean
Lovers of the season and of summer
Happiness and joy with faces full of smiles
Hand in hand, they walk tonight beneath the stars
The ocean waters come and go beneath their feet
Lovers kiss, lovers hugs, and caresses of the warm breeze
All beneath the blue starry night of summer
Kisses, kisses hug all through the warm night
They profess each other's summer love tonight
Blue the ocean, blue the starry skies with the new moon at night

Missing my Love

I miss you, love, I miss you more then ever. My life is like a void, no happiness inside me. I feel that you have gone somewhere without me. My love for you remained at home right here. You did not take it or take me with you. You told me that there'll be no tears again You took my writing, and you've gone and left me pain.

O, how I love you you'll never know! I lost you somewhere once more, annoyingly. How is your new love compared to mine? I can't see—my eyes are full of tears. My heart is broken and I don't want to live. It's emptiness without you; it is dark and cold. There is no life for me out there without you.

O, please, my love, just call my name so I will know that you are still somewhere. O, love, O, love, O, love of mine, there is no life without you anywhere.

October 2003

Where Are You

The thought of you put a smile on my face.
I wish I knew where you are, my love.
You are the green stone that was on my finger.
Where are you, love? Where are you, love?

At night the thought of you brings tears.
O, how I loved you for so long, you won't believe!
Your silliness with me, I did forgive, my love.
I cry for you—I can't find you, like you have told me.

Are you well, my love; is all going your way?
I wouldn't want it otherwise, my love.
Please send a word somehow, that I will know.
The holidays are here; I wish you well and luck.

The music plays, but you nowhere in sight.
It's not the same, my love, believe me, it is not.
You are the birthstone on my finger, love.
The tears just stream as I think of you, my love.

I wish, I wish, I wish so hard to see you, love.
There are no words invented to express that kind of love.
My dearest love, O, how much you are loved!
If only you did know, I'm sure you would return, my love.

The Firefly

In August 2003 on the front porch I sit
toward dusk on a warm evening.
As I sit I wait for nightfall and the moon,
for the few stars that will appear in the darkest skies.

A little firefly appears from the grassy area.
He starts hovering from grass to bush,
from bush to bush and over grass as he passes by my side.
As the darkness folds much thicker, I can see him dance.

More pronounced the firefly in flight from bush to grass—
a thought just crossed my mind, *catch the firefly and jar it.*
Then I thought of freedom, flight, and abandoned thought of capture,
but I continued my vigil on the flight of the firefly.

Darkness falls completely and the moon has appeared,
first quarter of the moon in dark, dark skies.
Few stars have flickered and the planes passed above the homes.
Stillness on my street—not a soul in sight or sound.

The firefly continues flying in his freedom dance.
I sit with out a motion, watching him flickering above the bushes,
over grass around me like a teasing dance,
Never-ending in his flight as he hovers or maneuvers over green.

Next morning I went out in search of the firefly that sleeps
but in the denseness of the leaves I could not find him.
I must wait till evening or nightfall to watch the firefly,
but as I wait in the evening he does not appear again.

February 2003

A Thought of God

As morning comes, the snow is falling.
The sun is out and bright today
but the snow continues falling.
It had covered trees and streets
like a beautiful white blanket or a bride.
Warmer inside the room today,
not as cold as yesterday.
As I lay and watch the snow
a thought of God crosses my mind.
O, how great and gracious you, almighty,
that you let me live so long!
Good or bad, I thank you most.
You have stood beside me for so long
as I walked and as I slept day in and day out.
Few things I understand, but most, I don't know why,
but I thank you kindly from the heart.
Thank you for the watch day in and night.
My faith in you I put my life, I give to you.

Waiting for Spring

On a glummest cold winter day,
I think of spring to come my way,
of all the dogwoods in their blossom
and the budding leaves of oak trees.

To walk in the botanical garden
among the roses that are abloom,
to walk beneath the arbors with the roses,
on the paths that are so green.

To cross into the Japanese garden
and watch all the turtles and the koi,
to walk in sunshine below the cloudless sky—
O, how impatient I became through winter!

But the winter is still with us and still cold,
but the thought of spring sunshine,
with its flowers all around it, and the green,
puts a smile on my face of pleasure.

I don't have to wait so long now; winter's almost over
and spring is around the corner.
All I have to do is wait a while for the budding to appear
and the flowers to come full bloom with sunshine.

January 2003

Yearning for Better Times

Not everything is beautiful in life
although I want it all to be.
I live in desolation, in a dark room,
A small room, with no sun that shines,
No sun to be seen at all, no sun at all.
My mood is down under like a storm,
A storm that won't pass so quickly.
My tears are like the rain in spring
and all that I can do is think of better,
of better times to come my way.
I wish that life was better, and the world at peace,
and peace is what I need to make it better,
better for the world in which I live my life.
Not everything is good or beautiful in life
although I want it all to be sunshine.
My yearning is tormenting me: tormenting.
And maybe it will pass, as it had come.
The sun will shine again, the storm gone,
once more I'll feel the beauty and the good.
The sun will shine again for me without the storm
and all will pass in one big dream.
I will wake up in beauty, and the life I know
I shall say that all is beautiful, and life goes on.

January 2003

Whispers

Whispers, whispers in the night
of promises of love to come,
whispers of the wind against the leaves,
the rushing water against dark skies,
whispers of longing that was,
whispers of longing for some one,
of promises of love to come.

Whispers of a loving, caring voice,
of dancing under the starry skies,
whispers of a dress that moves with dancing
under the full moon in the middle of the night,
longing whispers of some voice, familiar,
whispers of love to come some day.

Whispers, whispers among the flowers
in the midst of sunny day somewhere,
whispers of someone in love,
of love and promises to come,
whispers of some love long ago,
whispers of longing for someone.

January 2003

The Medallion

In my hand I held the golden boy medallion.
As I pulled the black ribbon of it, memories appeared,
memories of happy moments, of a curly golden boy,
tears started streaming like streams after a rain.

Memories at night of reading children stories,
 Dostoevsky's and *The Little Prince*
and much much more than just the memories,
but now I lost that golden boy to manhood.

Things are not as they used to be, all gone by, all gone.
The golden boy's no longer golden like the medallion in my hand,
No longer curly and golden like he was ages ago.
I can't dress him in a green tunic and give him a sword.

Slowly I pulled the black ribbon from the medallion,
folded it so my nightly tears won't wet it,
and the medallion lay beside me in a tiny little box.
I have stroked the image somewhat twice or more.

Where is the golden curly boy right now? I do not know.
So many memories, so many hugs and kisses,
but in my heart I know that he remembers me.
O, how I have adored you, little curly golden boy!

January 2003

Giving up Smoking

Once I used to sit so idle with a cigarette in hand,
wasting time all the way on smoke and nothing else,
thinking with a cigarette in hand for hours.
Nothing was accomplished, nothing was ever done.

Time wasted, money wasted on cigarettes and cough syrup,
coughing, coughing all night long, smoking all day long,
idle, very idle was I with a cigarette in hand.
Now I use the patches every day and I'm somewhat idle still.

But my money doesn't drain me and the coughing stopped.
Still, idle I became somewhat. Exercises I do.
I do not miss the cigarette at all; what a waste it was!
What prompted me to pick up a cigarette and smoke?

I gave up the smoking for good and ever more.
I'll get over my idleness somehow with time.
I don't miss you, cigarettes, I don't miss you, not a bit.
I have defeated the habit once and for all—you did not defeat me.

March 2003

Happiness

As I enter the dining room in the morning
the sun's rays are spreading through the window.
The illumination and the light is incredible.
Only nature can create such a thing.
It is indescribable—you have to see it.
It makes my heart leap and I'm happy all over.
My day has been made, no matter what will happen today,
I hold that happiness in my heart and don't let anything spoil it.
The sun warms the room, the rays spark like gold to light the gloom,
and I just bask in full happiness and joy.

Unhappy

Tired, tired, tired he looked,
unhappy, unhappy, unhappy he looked,
preoccupied, preoccupied he looked.
My heart went out to him.
My soul had started to suffer.
My mind did not let go of him.
Tired he looked and unhappy;
I suffer for him, and I don't even know why.

I uttered the first hello and a smile.
He became at ease and returned a smile.
How are you? he asked, *Are you fine?*
I'm fine, I answered and all under control.
He looked straight into my eyes with a smile,
but no longer did he look preoccupied.
No longer did he look so tired,
no longer did he look so unhappy as before.

I Hate Risperdal

I don't want to claw my way out like the rest.
I want it to come easy like it did in the past.
I'm so tired of taking the drug Risperdal
that kills all desire to create and to imagine.

Let them all climb and claw every day of their lives,
but for me it is freedom of drugs that I need.
But my doctor won't reduce my dose, not a bit.
Stern he is and reminds me that a hospital is in exchange.

I know that I don't want to be in the hospital once more,
but I do miss my feeling of creation and inspiration,
to write I cannot do well, to paint I cannot do at all.
Sometimes I say the hell with the Risperdal, and yet I take it.

I do not want to wind up in the hospital again.
I do not want to be questioned by strange doctors
but I do not want to claw like everyone else.
I do not want to struggle; everything came easy in the past.

Now I just sit think and smoke, idle.
Sometimes I'm not even able to finish a letter to a friend.
 I'm not inspired at all—I'm out of words—I have to claw,
and I don't now how to claw like the rest do.

I hate Risperdal, I hate Risperdal—it numbs me, it doesn't inspire.
In the past on a little of it, I was somewhat high but full of inspiration,
but now look at me—I'm dead all inside. I must claw my way out.
I hate Risperdal, I hate Risperdal. I can't find the medium in it.

To Live or Die

To live or die, that is the question
I ask myself so may times over.
To die, it comforts me so well,
and yet to miss on all the glory of tomorrow?
I ask you all what shall I do?
To die, it is so easy, like a blink,
but to live, it is so hard and heavy.
And yet to think that I will live no more?
It dampens all that I have thought so far.
To die, to live, to die, to live—what shall I do?
Please help me to decide, my friends.
The mood is gloomy now, but what about tomorrow?
If the sun will shine, I'll want to live.
To die or live, to die or live, I can't make up my mind.

No One to Love

There is no one to love in sight.
It is cold and windy tonight.
The winter is long and won't let go.
There are no tears for love, not near or far.

I used to cry for all my lovers.
My tears have streamed so hard
by now my eyes are dry. There is no love.
There is no love at all in sight.

My feelings all are numb and shut—
No tears, no love for anyone,
no lover, no regrets, no feeling.
Am I real or false right now?

Is it for good or just for a while?
Will I love again with passion as before?
Will I love with all of my desire
and compose the songs of love?

If only I could tell the future—
if only I could tell now for sure
that slowly I'd return to what I was,
I'd give all I have just to love again.

February 2004

Loneliness

Hard are the evening hours alone.
It's hard waiting for someone.
Long are the hours alone.
The dinner is ready and waiting.

Hard are the evening hours alone,
a cigarette in hand, some scribbling,
nothing to satisfy my mood,
no presence of a person in sight.

Hard are the evening hours alone.
At least during the day I'm not home.
Most of the time I'm out and about,
but evening comes and I'm all alone.

Hard are the evening hours alone
until he comes home and says hello,
and then *How was your day?* and in return, it was okay.
 Not much of a conversation.

But his presence eases all the pain.
The dinner ready, we eat together.
Small talk of this and that takes place
and finally the evening turns into night.

Feelings

O, the elated feelings, the ecstasy of all!
Compare it to today's dead feelings
or the rage and hate that I expressed.
I feel so dead inside without these feelings.
O, how I miss elated feelings and the ecstasy of all!
In the past my feelings were ecstatic and profound
and today I'm dead and won't shed a tear for anyone.
Or is just not intense enough to feel like ecstasy?
O, ecstasy please return to me or elated feelings.
O, the elated feelings the ecstasy of all!
Please make me feel alive and whole again.

A Chapter is Closing

A chapter is closing in my life.
He did not cure me
but he made me sane again.
Nothing is left, no imagination to write,
no talent to paint,
nothing but struggle ahead.

There are no highs, there are no lows,
just an even mood that gets nowhere.
The mind clear, there are no voices.
There are no stories to be told,
There are no visions to be painted.

There is no music, there are no colors.
It's a bland, ordinary world out there.
I'm sane. my mind quiet, and I'm boring.
I have so little to say.
 I listen and I look, but nothing is exciting.

Every thing I try is just a struggle,
but he made me sane again,
ordinary, not great, not patient, but sane.
I try to paint—it's not so great.
I try to write—the word don't flow or rhyme.

I don't give up. A day goes by, I try again,
and as I try, I say maybe this is it.
O, Lord, I wish it were, I try so hard,
But nothing—just a struggle with a glimpse of hope—
and all I need is just a little hope.

Farwell, Mama

Morning glory, sunshine, Mother's warmth—
come day, come evening, Mother's there.
O, how it hurts, O, how I feel Mother's comfort near.
Bad days, good days come and go, but Mother's here.

As we grow and turn away, Mother steadfast stands.
She counsels, she discusses and displays,
the disappointments and the hurts she takes away.
She comforts and she loves us to a sacrifice.

Then we leave her and she is alone.
We forget her love and sacrifices and all she stood for,
busy, busy with our lives, too busy to remember Mother—
oops, until a hurt appears, until a disappointment surfaces.

Now we have a family, we need our mother dear.
We need the love, the care, the knowledge, and the safety.
Our children care for our mother dear and
once again we look for love and comfort in her arms.

Mother, dear, don't get old, stay young and care for me,
but Mother doesn't listen and gets old and helpless.
 Morning turns into night, the sun into the moon,
blue skies into clouds, summer into winter.

Winter comes for Mother, helpless as she is.
A child she is, and now is our turn to love her.
We care for her, take her pain away, give her hope,
but winter is harsh, the trees are naked, the air is cold.

Mother, dear, keep on living, don't give up,
She is in a dream, in a beautiful childish dream.
She utters a word—I love you very much—O, how I know
that you took so many pains away!

O, morning glory, O, sunshine, O, day—
stay one more day, try—don't slip away.
But Mother's dream is stronger than us.
She is in a deep sleep, a peaceful sleep, like forever night,

So we say farewell, Mama, farewell,
thanks for all the morning glories, for all the sun,
for all the parties and gatherings you did,
for all the children that you brought up.

All the hearts and disappointments that you healed—
we loved you then, we love you now,
and we thank you for the sunshine, no mater how small or how big.
Peace upon you, love be with you, from all of us.

Note:
Written for Mom's Memorial service on May 30, 2007

Harsh Voice

Talking down to myself
Talking harsh and stern
Never pressing never giving
Never praising or forgiving
Talking, talking, to myself
O Jill, if you could hear me now
I stop; I don't put myself down
O no, no more critics for me
But my inner voice just goes on
Stop I say, stop right now
Would I speak like that to others?
O no, never would I dare
But I'm talking to myself
I'm talking harsh and stern
I'm putting myself down,
Jill; please help me, once again
Just the thought of you
Stops me in my mind

I Cry in Silence

My soul is crying, my mood is black.
I'm lamenting over art, over what I cannot do.
My breast is heavy, my emotions are aflame,
my mind not at ease, it's overactive with the thought:
What holds me back, I do not know or why.
The easel stands, the canvas on, the painting is unfinished.
I cannot touch it or approach it, just look at it with desperation.
Six months have passed and I'm still not finished.
So simple, so unpretentious and uncomplicated,
but I cannot approach it, cannot pick up a brush.
I look and heaviness of mind overtakes me once again.
I'm quiet, not one outburst and no protest. I have to finish it,
but how? My mind is numb, my mood is dark and low,
I'm alone: my mind is a scramble with emotions,
How long is it going to last this time—a day, a week, a month?
I'm at a loss, there is no one, I'm alone with all my pain and agony.
I cry inside for help, for comfort and understanding or some inspiration.

A Friend for a Day

Saturday, my soul was singing.
I was flying above the clouds.
I was inspired, my heart was light, my mind at ease.
The future seemed to be so clear and light.
The laughter, O, the laughter! My heart was light.
You eased the heaviness and all confusion
You shared some moment of your pain and longing for your mother.
You showed me kindness and gave me hope.
I shall remember you as one that has a soul,
as the angel that you are.

Cindy

Now I'm down and distressed; anxiety sets in—what to do?
I call you, my dear Cindy, at all times of the day.
You lend me you ear; you calm me down with your voice.
O, how I bother you each day, with my trivial matters,
And you so patient toward me, so kind and understanding.
You have your problems too, but you never let them on to me.
You save each day for me, from loneliness and boredom.
O, how I love you for what you are—the angel of my soul.
O, how I appreciate each thing you do for me each day.
There are no words to praise you.
There are no prizes to be won for all your goodness.
Kindness is engraved in you for good.
My little angel that you are, you'll never know how much I love you.

When I am Lonesome

O, Karl dear, I have to hear a voice.
O, dear, are you working? Are you free?
I'm going crazy, and I have to talk.
There is no one out here but me.
I must speak to someone.
I have to hear the voice of someone.
How are you, dear, are you okay?
I painted something small today.
It's not too great, but not too bad.
Okay, I know you have to go
but thank you for the moment.
I love you much, my son, for listening to me.

Before The Inheritance

I did not want you to wait for me to die. I wanted you to have it now while I'm alive, to adorn you with all the finest that I have, so you enjoy it now while you are young. It is from me to you as warm remembrance, so use it well and use it as often as you can. With all my love and gratitude to you, my dear, adorn your little neck to show the world that you have status like them all and more.

The Birthday

Today is my sixty-second birthday.
Anticipation grows toward evening hours.
My son, my granddaughter and her boyfriend,
My grandson and his girl, are all invited.
Should I bejewel myself, or stay simply elegant?
What should I wear? It's hot today.
I did my hair; I did my makeup too.

I know! I'll put on a pure white dress,
high heels, a see-through shawl—
I look a million dollars, for the evening.
It's a warm evening, how is driving?
To bad my older son and wife are away
but what fun it is to be among the young.
Anticipation grows to the evening hours

We gathered at the restaurant, all pretty.
I was presented with long stemmed mixed roses.
We were greeted with a smile and were seated.
My husband ordered wine, one bottle after another.
The conversation flowed, the giggles and the laughter.
The food arrived, the praises for the chef,
and who did what today and what we'll do tomorrow.

The restaurant had emptied of all patrons.
The place became my private room.
I kept the conversation going till dessert
And then I said without discretion, *Picture time!*
Please, waiter, take a picture of all of us,
a picture of you two and of you two and of you,
and now a picture for posterity of me and George.

Slowly the evening passed and the dinner was over.
Lazily every one go up, hugs and kisses.
There was a line of idle waiters waiting to leave.
The music played, but the place was empty.
We walked out and waved good-bye and said good night.
As I got in to the car I thought how wonderful it was,
How full of life the evening was, how lucky and how blessed, I am.

Pumpkin Soup on Canvas

Early in September morning
to the market I went
for something to buy for dinner.
To my surprise I saw pumpkins.

Overwhelmed by their sizes,
by the shapes and colors,
greedily I bought a few.
As I paid, I thought, *soup tonight!*

On the way home, my imagination stirred.
Emotions overtook all senses.
Excitement overtook me by surprise:
 I shall make a painting of these pumpkins.

As I got home, I set up the pumpkins.
the tureen, the knife, the ladle, and went on painting.
The time lapsed unnoticed; evening had arrived.
What about my soup? I thought, *it's on canvas now.*

And that is how my painting started,
with great caution and precision,
I did apply the paint
and the thought of soup appeared in mind, once or twice
but what is food compared to something lasting?

I Woke Up Again

The day was cold but glorious.
The sun was spreading its rays all over.
To paint I have prepared myself today.
My doctor has reduced the medication by one mg.

The canvas on the easel,
the picture is outlined in the paint.
Slowly as I squeeze the paint onto the palette,
I see how vivid are the colors.

Brushes are in hand.
I choose one, I dab it in the paint,
 I swirl it around, I dab it into another paint and mix it
onto the canvas—what amazement!

What a color just like life itself!
Am I awake or am I dreaming?
I continue on; the peaches come alive.
I want to take one—I want to bite into one.

When I finish they are so real,
I wonder if the rest is going to be real.
Does one mg of medication make such difference?
It woke me up from my deep sleep.

I see colors, vivid colors.
I can mix them and mach them.
I see all details that I have missed in the past.
I woke up from a deep sleep of five long years.

I can paint again—I can feel the colors!
I'm alive again, I'm happy again,
I'm at ease with my art again,
I'm awake with happiness in my life again.

God's Gift

As I get older I think of you a lot.
I turn to you for comfort and appreciation,
but most of all I want to thank you for the gift,
the gift that you bestowed upon me.

As I stand or sit and paint,
I enter into a world of wonder,
A world that is so beautiful and calm,
All worries disappear—creation is the thought.

And as I paint I think how blessed I am
that you bestowed such gift upon me,
to make such beauty for eternity to come,
known or unwoven creation is my strength.

I have been inspired lately more than one can think.
Excited I became that I could paint again.
Such wonder and such colors are beyond me,
a true gift, a gift not to take for granted.

A gift that I must pursue for time to come.
You blessed me with such a gift.
I make so many people around me happy,
and most of all, my heart is full of happiness and gratitude.

Little Hands Holding a Peach

Peaches, sweet peaches
Summer's fruit, summer's memory
Little feet running in the orchard
Little hands picking peaches

Summer's breezes, summer's sunshine
Ripe peaches in the baskets
Little hands collecting peaches
Ripe peaches, sweet peaches

Little girl sitting in a chair
Little hands holding a large peach
Summer's bounty, summer's memory,
Sweet peaches in the summer sunshine

Memories of bounty, memories of summer
Memories, sweet memories of peaches
Little hands holding a big peach
Little girl sitting in the orchard in sunshine

The Butterfly

O, Mother dear, you always wanted to come back as a butterfly.
I painted a butterfly for you one day that I had seen
atop some cliff upstate among some wildflowers in midday.
 They were in flight so delicate and yet so graceful.

You were so beautiful and graceful during life.
I called you in a secret *la nymph* because of the way you were.
The butterflies just hover over flowers up and down,
capturing my gaze. I wonder where they came from and where they go.

A dance of grace and mystery upon them in between the flowers,
the sunrays only intensify their look and beauty beyond description.
If you could come back as a butterfly, would you hang around my garden?
If only you could see the butterfly I painted just for you.

Ode to Dr. David Roane

You saved my life, you gave me peace,
you brought me back from darkness to the light.
I praise you with a song of gratitude and love
from the healing you have done for me.

Such love and care are rare today,
but you persisted and devoted all your might
to heal my mind and my soul from all confusion.
I sing a song of all devotion to my savior.

I praise your name among the kings of kings,
among the wise, the kind, and the just.
Rough was the road to my recovery but you persisted;
you never gave up hope on me, not once.

I have a special place in my heart and mind just for you.
You are the wise one, the kind one, the patient one.
You never tired of my illness. You brought me love.
I sing praise to you each day and night.

A song of all of my devotion to your existence,
a song so sweet that angels sing with me.
Without you I never would have been here.
My praises are not enough for what you did.

I Must Go First

I have lived a full life so far—
an interesting one, at that—
and if I'll be gone tomorrow,
 I'm not afraid at all of it.

But you, my love, I'm worried.
The thought of you not being here,
It frightens me beyond compare.
The loneliness, the void, to be without you.

Without you there will be no laughter.
There will be no news of worldly happenings.
There will be no morning to wake up to,
no evenings to anticipate excitement.

There will be no love, no care.
Please stay a while longer here with me.
Don't let me worry over you.
The fright is real as day and night.

Without you there will be darkness,
no kind words or encouragement,
no comfort of your thoughts out loud,
no smile when I'm sad to cheer me up.

Please stay a while longer just for me.
Take care—don't let me lose you!
I must be going first.
That way I won't know suffering.

Jill

I came to you for help.
I didn't know what to expect.
You made it easy, you eased my mind.
You counseled me and wiped my tears.

You taught me strength of mind—
how to be assertive and be kind.
You brought me order that I lacked
and gave me strength to go ahead.

You taught me courage and some love,
how I must pursue my goals each day.
You cleared the clutter in my mind
and encouraged me to be myself.

You took all negative thought away from me.
You taught me to be better person with myself.
You brought sunshine when it rained
and when it stormed in my life, you calmed it all.

What can I say? There is just one like you,
the one who loves humanity so well
and helps to my delight.
Without you, my being would be shattered.

There are no words to praise you or your work.
There are no prizes to be given for your advice,
but one thing I know—a better person I became,
and all of that it is because of you, my dear Jill.

You led me straight; you never failed me.
You picked me up when I stumbled.
I wouldn't know what to do without you.
Only you could solve all of my problems.

And yet you are so modest for your doing.
My joy is yours each time when I succeed.
The fruit of your labor of love is showing.
Now I do remember what you say to me and I repeat

There is one Jill and not another in this world.
The caring and the nurturing she is.
You helped me through and through each time.
You are one of a kind on this earth.

My Grandson Karl

My grandson Karl, a college he is attending,
a graduate of military school he is,
a gentlemen and considered and kind he is.
A girl he has; running around with her he does.

Karl calls me to inquire to my being,
To make a date for breakfast or to see me.
He is an inspiration to my soul and mind,
Great support and encouragement in moments of defeat.

Karl is eighteen but wise beyond compare.
Conversation he can hold all on his own.
Proud grandmother I am about my grandson,
loving, caring, and observing everything around.

Painting he does, wonderful for his age!
Friends he has had since he was small.
Work he does after school in a health spa,
but he always finds time for his grandma.

I Know a Woman Named Mila

I have known you since I'm forty-seven.
Now I'm sixty-two and still you are the same.
Each week I came to you for manicure,
you greeted me wholeheartedly and spoke so softly.

You spoke to me in a language of the poets,
the language of my mother tongue, Russian.
I have practiced it with you and have improved.
You were so genteel and so caring all along.

There was no criticism or putting down.
There was always caring in you.
How many times have you made me happy?
Happy when I was so sad and unsure of myself?

And now, when one day you were seriously ill—
it was life or death now for you, dear Mila—
but you have taken it in stride with lots of hope.
You took the illness with your myth and won your life.

Not once did you complain about discomfort.
The treatments that you got were rough,
but you, dear Mila, have survived it all—
with courage and in silence you went ahead.

And yet you served me in spite of yourself
and still you comforted me when I was sad.
I do admire you, your courage, and your spirit—
the aura that you spread illuminates your being.

How unselfish and how kind have you been to me!
I would not change you for another or for all the gold!
Your life became so dear to me and so important—
you are courageous—live a long and happy life. I love you, Mila.

Dr. Blye

She is a woman first of all,
a gentle soul, serene and pleasant.
She always greets me with a smile
and wants to know how I have been.

She speaks ever so softly
with confidence and knowledge.
She doesn't miss anything.
She eases all my tension and my mind.

I'm reassured that I'm all right
when I'm ill or don't feel good,
that all will pass—not to worry.
She helps to overcome all worries.

I've known her for years by now.
She has remained the same.
Her mood never changes toward me.
Her kindness, the same, her voice still soft.

There should be more like her—
helpful, pleasant, understanding,
so ever genteel, Dr. Blye.
She is not afraid to show her caring.

My Friend Victoria

How many years have passed since we first met?
How many things have happened in our lives since then?
But you, my friend, remained the same as always,
my friend through thick and thin, through illness and despair.

You stood by me, never to have flinched aside.
As I remember, basket in your hand, a long hallway.
In a hospital I was—you came, no questions asked,
a long way from your home—you made the trip.

And as the years went by and closer we became,
a soul mate you became, an artist like I am,
a photographer you are, who captures images for all time.
You captured all my work and more.

You help without a question, you oblige me in all ways.
That kind of a friendship is not easy to find anywhere.
You are my friend, the only one to whom I can truly say
I think of you with love and fondness, and appreciation, too.

No More Sorrow for Myself

Feeling low, feeling unworthy, no one is in sight,
never good enough or even pretty anymore.
Where are my accomplishments? They're gone.
What have I become so far today?

And then it struck me by surprise—
enough of sorrow, enough of that for now.
I'm worth it, I'm as good as anyone
and maybe better if I think about it hard.

Tomorrow I will paint and every day,
no matter what, it will come out—some scribbles?
Some mystery on canvas to display for a crowd?
I'll show them all my worth and then we'll see.

I know that I can do it if I want; I must.
No obstacle is in my way. I have the time and the day.
I must, I cannot, let the sorrow swallow me.
The sun is shining every morning now each day.

Just do it, don't think about it for too long.
Tomorrow is near, the night just separates it.
No more sorrow for yourself, you're worth it.
You are as good as anyone—or even better.

Red Wine

Wine from a distant land of hills and mist,
a land of sunshine, fertile soil, warm breezes,
mysterious wine—long forgotten the year and the label,
mysterious like a woman of worldly knowledge and experience.

Wine, red wine, in the bars, the clubs, the restaurants,
On dinner tables has been poured, red like blood and aromatic.
Taste it slowly—smell it first, thick the wine, red like blood.
With each swallow excitement overtakes you—warm is the feeling

With each swallow you want more, wine, red wine, thick and lush.
Now you yearn for some more, for the goodness of red wine.
The mysterious bottle that you had is almost gone—no more—
like a vanishing beautiful, illusive woman that was here and gone.

Wine, red wine, in the bars, in the clubs, the restaurants,
on the dinner tables, in the cellars of the vineyards.
Pour it and drink it up, swirl it around, smell it—
red, red wine, only a memory and the warm feeling left.

My Only Brother, Sergei

We were born in a faraway land,
Father taken in our youthful days.
Hand in hand we walked through wars—
from land to land we wandered on.

My soul mate you became,
protecting me from all I feared.
My brother you have been as always,
my trust I put in you not only once.

You bailed me out in situations big and small.
You guided me not only once to better ways
and still you were my brother through thick and thin.
We marched through darkest nights to reach the light.

You never abandoned me
and when I needed you, you came.
You, still my brother as before and always,
I'll stand by you through thick and thin like you.

I have one brother who I love,
a brother that I care for more than me.
My heart is full of gratitude for all you did.
One brother do I have—I held his hand through youth.

Granddaughter Natasha

She shies away from me in company of friends,
grown up and independent, free spirit of the times,
never looking back, just forward as she strides,
turning up on front door steps—*Surprise, Grandma!*

Not one minute does she sit at home—
always on the move and prowling about.
Serious she can be for one minute, I may say.
Going places, working, working, studies, studies.

Kind, gentle, full of fury, temper, temper,
loving, caring, but no time to waste.
I shall see you, Grandma, when or where I do not know.
There's no time to be wasted, going places, places, places.

There is a Girl I Know

There is a lovely girl I know so well.
so pretty, so friendly, and so loving.
Once she was a scatterbrain—
today she is all seriousness and looks ahead.

Her future was so dim and foggy,
but it reversed itself for good.
She studies, works, and helps.
Once she was so outspoken

But today she weighs her words.
The girl I knew has changed completely.
Earnest she is goodness she has.
She promises success—I'm sure of that.

The girl I know is kind and so loving.
I'm proud to know her well.
I brag about her all the time.
I love her to no end to come.

The Song

Sitting by a sunny window while guitars are serenading,
golden voice is sounding so seductive and alluring.
Emotion overtake me and is coming to the fore right now.
Warm feeling has engulfed the early morning mood.

The serenading wailing sound of guitars goes on.
The voice is sounding far away and fading slowly.
O, how comforting that sound and the song was!
O, how sensual and wonderful the wailing of guitars!

Sound by the sunny window in the morning,
O, the wailing of guitars and golden voice—
a song of long ago that brought emotions forward.
It stirred me up for new desires that overtook me.

Suddenly all mattered once again in life.
The sun was shining through the window on the flowers
and the silence fell upon the room.
The song had ended as it had began but, O, the wailing of guitars!

My Cousin, My Sister Lydia

I have a brother but not a sister
until you came from far away.
You brought me friendship and good will.
We mingled with each other every day.

We parted and departed through the years.
Your visits were heartwarming and a joy.
I remember the trip to Paris still so well,
all the exploring and running around we did.

So free, so carefree in your care,
the mornings we spent reminiscing of the past,
the secrets no one will know—
how easy it is to put my heart out to you.

If only you knew how much you mean to me
and how much you are thought of each day.
The days we spent were not all in vain.
A cousin you are, but a sister you became.

Fall

Yellow orange brown leaves
Pale sun and cool breezes
Grass from green to yellow brown
Rains that won't let go for days
Early darkens in the evenings
Cozy corner on the couch to read
After long walks in the streets
Not for long the beauty of the earth shall be—
Soon the earth will go to sleep

A Contradiction

Fresh food organic food no hormones no antibiotics
Exercises each day breathe fresh air lots of sunshine
Just a little meat more fish chicken and vegetables
No more three cups of coffee—green tea instead

Yogurt every day lots of vegetables and fruit—and
then desire creeps upon my soul real slowly
and an inner fight takes place within my mind
but desire overtakes all reason

Desire is so strong that I forget all promises—I say
just this time just one today and no more.
I light a cigarette and think my lungs my heart
Why do I observe all things healthy, yet I smoke?

My Argument about a Saying

Why do they say old people reach a golden age?
The golden age belongs to people in the middle of their lives.
It's full of golden light, travel, and delights,
desires being reached, health, and friends abounding.
Golden sun shines between the youth and aged one.
I say the old ones have reached the age of silver.
It's gray, it's cold, it's lonely, full of pain and memories.
Few want you, few love you, and some are even quite repelled.
A piece of silver that you love in youth lays forgotten in the drawer.
That is how old age is, and you can't recover youth.
I compare the end years to silver—it is cold as granite underfoot,
and then they are laid in the cold ground like that silver is found in,
cold like granite beneath the foot of passerby.
The start is warm, nurturing, and caring—the middle is all gold and sun—
the end is gray as silver in its coldness,
and then it is the end.

Adieu

When I was young I was among you.
I flourished and I grew with you.
I traveled far and near to see the world.
I had the pleasure of your company at hand.

As the time went by and by,
I got older, then, you know,
I drifted far from you.
I memorized times past.

Good fellows and good cheers,
the ladies are a memory to cherish,
the parties are a dream to dream,
all memories inscribed inside me.

Now I must part from you, my friends,
I take a different road ahead to follow
new dreams to dream, new friends to make.
My time was, and now is past.

With sorrow and good will I part from you.
I shall remember every one from past till now.
Good luck to all; may all your dreams come true.
Adieu, farewell, good-bye—the pleasure was all mine.